# BOOK OF THE GIVEN

# BOOK OF THE GIVEN

## RUSTY MORRISON

Noemi Press
Las Cruces, New Mexico

LIBRARY OF CONGRESS CATALOGING-IN-PUBLICATION DATA

Morrison, Rusty.

Book of the given / Rusty Morrison. — 1st ed.

    p. cm.

Poems.

ISBN 978-1-934819-09-8

I. Title.

PS3613.O7777B66 2010

811'.6 — dc22

                        2010030888

COVER ART

Nan Parsons, "Dreaming of Water" (detail)

Oil, 48" x 39"

www.nanparsonsart.com

Published by Noemi Press, Inc., a nonprofit literary organization

www.noemipress.org

*for Ken*

# CONTENTS

in assuming that the other is the same, one reduces the other to the self,
one takes from the other,
and "deliberately and recklessly brush[es] the dust off the wings
of the butterfly that is called the moment"

Rosalyn Diprose, quoting Nietzsche

ASSEMBLED FROM THE SCRIPT: BATAILLE

No chapel, no wounded-soldier-in-the-last-scene sacrament,

no field of windswept grass where lovers walk

as the background music swells to tell us

*full communication resembles flames — the electrical*


fence already surrounds your found object,

which I'm too afraid to fondle. I'd be pitting water against glass.

I have only to imagine you

in my hands, and my skin is a pox of impact,

while the wild horse silhouetted on the sun-blanched horizon

merely kicks hooves and we swoon to that

*discharge of lightning. Its attraction*


too flawless.

I am nearly sick with child-haste.

Where have I put her this time? Doll in a box. Doll

in my lips, belly, breasts?

She's gone.

What will I offer you now? Nervous as a kneeling supplicant

at the bishop's door. Bishop

in both of us, brooding, turning

his eyes round me as though I were the trick of perspective.

Every object I am

*is the rupturing it is built on*


—still you don't understand, though I come dressed

in several hints. My little song-skirt, call it

rhythm-to-tear-its-own-seams with,

set to the tone poem of odorous ripening. I make you

a little noise in my throat, under-heard,

*which increases its intensity in proportion to*


my feigned disinterest.

While you watch the mesmerizing spin
of a bikewheel that's just tumbled us, muddy,
into a roadside ditch
that had hidden from us
*its depth.*


The script: *full communication resembles flames — the electrical discharge*
*of lightning. Its attraction is the rupturing it is built on, which increases*
*its intensity in proportion to its depth*

UNSCRIPTED / 1

**Exposing the seen: a book of snapshots**


Beware nostalgia's elaborate snare—its tempting surfaces of gloss will tighten time around us. Each morning, I hold aloft an infant image of us, as you baptize her new again. Let stillness fall from her, I chant, ripen her vulnerability. The revival music you are playing on our old jukebox is luring an unusual number of souls from my secret neighborhood.

**Before generosity is possible, expectation must be abandoned**

There's no starlight to obscure the inflammation of pure sky tonight. I keep my fingernails cut close enough to follow change with my fingertips. Fog knows best how to test the approximating line of intimacy. The shiver that could be my next start at life—find me. In even this thick alpaca scarf. Only later, deciphered your distance-filled glance as lambent. Any interpretation is shaped by the ways I arrange my selves around it. When I close my eyes, I see there's no pattern for what pattern interrupts.

**A distance the given can draw upon**

An experiment in hurrying nothing into memory, a thickness to treat delicately, a chilled honey allowed to orb between thumb and forefinger, so long as I don't draw upon it with too much force. Then, with too much force, what can it matter, since no memory is ever completely lost. We know this, the experts tell us. The wall between this room and the next. Put there to steady us. Still, I want to work it. There are vertebrae in each form of forgetfulness that might want alignment, the gentlest tests of pressure and breath.

# SENTENCED BY THE SCRIPT: BATAILLE

Guilt, the innermost muscle pulling skin taut as a sentinel

I mistake for prayer.

Your silence, your wordlessly moving lips

strip all pageantry from my continent.

Turn on the news, let commerce construct of us

its uniform no one

on this vagrantly various screen. Or we go out,

to linger at café tables—you talk of sex, I nurse

a little welt of cigarettes and lips, Paris

and hand-wrapped chocolates.

*Eroticism as seen by the objective intelligence*


might be the parting folds of a coat, taken off in the rain,

under the weight of wandering

any landscape.

The way my hand must remove its layer of invisibility
to touch your face. I want to touch it.
To make that want, to meet it
*is something monstrous, just like religion. Eroticism and religion*

fill the space I try to befriend with a word like "body."
Not "liver," "lung."
My breasts I pretend are two birds we watched
close their wings and dive
through the story I make of sky at dusk. All the hours of dusk
*are closed books to us if we do not*

plunge into the silence that most frightens us.

No word to draw out

the dark flock

of our threat. Inside the flock,

only vibrations intone where we might stroke.

Your hand on my belly's skin,

and my dead—who are they? faceless as sex—will rise to it.

Nothing

of the clarity in a mirror's glass, which would

*locate them firmly in the realm of inner experience.*


The script: *Eroticism as seen by the objective intelligence is something monstrous, just like religion. Eroticism and religion are closed books to us if we do not locate them firmly in the realm of inner experience.*

UNSCRIPTED / 2

**The given is restive in gesture**


We ask each other repeatedly, *what am I worth*, a coercion that is as answerless as it is invidious. But no weather is actually monotone. Yesterday's soothing fog is today's blight of cracking knuckles and seemingly beneficent offers. Cunningly flawed, no form of touching is speechless in the movie version I rented so that we needn't discuss it again.

## Generosity resists clandestine promises


Orders coming in from 'the understood'. Beautiful, cloud-fed, silk-draped declarations, offering us the means to master this moment. Magisterial, easy to oblige. Orders nonetheless. Courage arrives wordlessly, with as yet unknown signatories. The Young King must teach himself valor for his pose under the fleur-de-lis canopy. I say that I'd trade the velvet-cloaked princess-concentrate for a more breathable air. But saying is so easily capitulated inside my head. Every pronouncement should be stamped on my local sky, visible and indisputable as halo. Only in paintings, you reply. I remember a willow-lined path, done in oils, hanging above my grandmother's couch — but not how to explain the halo it held for me. If you won't arrest me for my manipulations of scale, I won't make a prison for you with my listening. Today, I will not play the game of large, docile eyes, the kind that dark eye-liner is meant to emphasize.

**Scenes within the seeing**

I was ready for rain, but this morning's cloudlessness is entirely blue in answer. And you are quick to converse in cerulean. I have no reply. Sky, I could say. But would this be mere abeyance? Simply biding my time. Such an elemental shift must wear its own wings. Anise swallowtail, fluttering now, on the otherwise subject-less slope. Approach, and it offers the precision of vanishment that I see daily in your face, in my own. What are you thinking? I ask. My thoughts woven of the same event as yours, but with photons forming atoms into an entirely different cloth. Squint, when a brilliant morning vestments us both. The shock is a kind of smile.

PSALM FOR THE SCRIPT: BATAILLE

Not "God" whispered in our shared darkness

where herdsmen run helplessly behind the stampeding flock

painted on a domed roof that cracks open to expose

a further unfolding

star-blasted hemisphere already disappearing

on the screen of closed lids, after I recall myself

back into my eyes.

Not

that hushed, abjectly beseeching

cry.

But the dare—

did you speak it? I hear the bare soles of our feet running

from the sound—

that what we call to, facing each other, is

"No one."

*Unless the taboo is observed with fear, it lacks*


the tether that holds thumb to forefinger, hammer to nail,

black dog to white dog as they run

the new scent down through alleys—elastic, invisible membrane

that draws to danger

*the counterpoise of desire, which gives it its*


god over the game.

Complicit in each vexed visitation, haven't I
cultivated my own captivity? Persuaded myself of its
*deepest significance. The worst of it is*

feeling the weight of hips, belly, thighs,
regardless of my struggle to rise
from the planet.
As though I could move up a grassy mountain
from my body to yours.
Same failure, that I must break a law,
if I am ever to live by it,
*that science, whose procedures demand an objective approach to*

night-herons rising behind my closed eyes,
as your eyes watch.
Situating ourselves in any object
is always a threat. Pretend instead
that words can make a humanness between us.
That hand as "hand"
might hold us,
a little longer. I reach for your hands, knowing that
*taboo owes its existence to them but*

I want your fingers
to push my hair back, exposing my face.

I need you to hold my shoulders as doves
to release and then watch
return of their own volition
to your grasp.
And the floor teeters obediently — naïve, sweet,
corruptible senses. Whatever enlivens
*at the same time disclaims them because taboos are*

"this," "that," "your," "my" — whatever directive we use
to distill the salt of sentience,
though it tests the tongue with its acrid
*not-rational.*

The script: *Unless the taboo is observed with fear it lacks the counterpoise*
*of desire, which gives it its deepest significance.*
*The worst of it is that science,*
*whose procedures demand an objective approach to taboo,*
*owes its existence to them*
*but at the same time disclaims them because taboos are not rational.*

UNSCRIPTED / 3

**Generosities difficult to discern**

The weight of the palm of my hand, for instance, instead of a comforting word. Some offers have all the force of forgetfulness. Yet we each recognize even the subtlest indifference. Which is to say gifts can never be given back. How often I step between difficult questions even as my positions expand. I sit by the lake watching paper boats swell with the substance they were built to sail across, and then they drown. So there's always another direction to travel in, I imagine you saying without trace irony. If we would just open our eyes when we're in it, I'd reply, without trace competition.

**Each scene, its own microclimate**


Into the gap between good destiny and bad, we throw our choices. Do not call them mistakes. I look into your face. This containment of our mortal business. I glimpse a small pulling-together of your brows, which argues against your causal mouth. Who is to say what colors the lens of each least gesture? There are no repeat visitations. The months have names, but they don't answer when we call them to come back. We've been producing again, when what we need is to drive to the woods and walk. Douglas fir. Red trillium. Purple tufted thistle. Idea, in its deteriorating orbit. Dense moisture, smoking from tall patches of moss. Thick kinds of looking, without memory. I am not necessary to my own revelation, only to the monitoring of its brief interval.

**The given confounds**


After several attempts, my smile calms down. Exposing its valor as pretence. And then the frightening cost of quiet, which is a function of its glamour. No matter how closely I watch your hand move toward mine, several of its emotions I miss. Memory, for instance. The way it hides us, but only from ourselves. Which is not to ignore the use of accuracy as distraction, or the explanation that I shouldn't have started, already rearranging. Perhaps. But what can anyone really tell? Just-born giraffes drop as far as six feet. Life still catches them. Cleaning out the junk drawer, I find all the rubber bands are still young and elastic.

FACELESS BEFORE THE SCRIPT: BATAILLE

We are not calm tonight, but creaturely with quiet
amassing between us
the one direction that two bodies breed,
a close-walled, convulsive passage —
*eroticism is a ghastly maze where*

the body knows no one

can follow it

into the earth

of its innermost workings, into the matter (do not call it death)

that flesh eventually will find

itself becoming in its final loss

of the way toward touch. How, in that last awareness,

*the lost ones must tremble. This*


failure is ancient

with intoxicants—the orphan I am, warming her hands

before your huntsman fire,

its burn-marks still dark

on ground where you stand to collect from night sky

the numbers that teach you to count out the value

of a gold cup you can fill

with the certainty

that my lips will desire to drink from it.

Though every image we hold of the other drifts into static,

something of that electricity always in my hands

as I touch you,

a shock, like all of landscape suddenly

deranged of perspective,

untying its allegiance to meaning's order,

exactly opposite, but equal

to the pleasure that fills a child when she first learns to tie

the bows on her white shoes. To hand each other

these loosened strings

*is the only way to come close to eroticism: to tremble.*


The script: *eroticism is a ghastly maze where the lost ones*
*must tremble. This is the only way to come close to eroticism: to tremble*

UNSCRIPTED / 4

**Generosities won't line up to be counted**

You are watching me. The chiming interior of my answer, if sifted through the common public, will make no sound. Why do I feign a socially-sanctioned smile? Like trying to balance on one leg. Imbecilic and difficult at once. Why go as a stick-figure into my own fear in order to answer your fleshed silence? If we measure each choice—move closer, talk, don't talk—we will only master equivalence. Every clock tick will be the next picket in the fence between us, if I let each glance between us beget in me a new superstition. Instead, I will ignore all of our previous pronunciation aides, and let the animal tell us it is the animal.

**Versions of the seen**

I am drawing your face from memory. Leaving spaces for the stones I've not classified, will not find. Granite striates the outcroppings at Half Dome, this is a decade past. Pillow basalt along the Coast Range of Jenner; where either of us might have been the one falling, while the other called it future, throwing pebbles. You are facing the violence of gesture that I record in absolutely motionless gravel, which is fine-grained and extrusive, and into which you will not be drawn. Every style of line I amass must be valued, or the reproduction will disappear. We call that embedding. Layers of bedded lava are glassy, almost translucent, due to rapid cooling, forced to the surface. This shard of rhyolite, milk-white with pink overtones, this flattery, and the negative space in which the flattery fails. Everything plays a part. Every fissure I draw, filled only with smoke, is the survival of some missed attention looking back emptily at the viewer.

**Generosities not easily shared**

There are no strategies in the good will of objects. I want to sit beside you, looking you in the eye, as close as that. Which means not looking past the point where it becomes only looking that is looking back. Left with room enough, we might witness how much our own interior distances demand of us. There was an apple in the branches of my dream, going the long way on its own to ripeness. Reaching ruined it.

BETOKEN THE SCRIPT: BATAILLE

This whiteness—teeth of a moment,
bared.
Or just the white of our bare skin.
Do you sense it?
Vibrational, like a growl low in the throat. What
*chance summons*

we can't be taught to hear.

We ask for a catechism

to teach breasts, thighs, knees. Ink

of the real, a line

to follow the rise and fall of breath.

I want to fix a meaning in the pressure of my hand

against your chest—

as though it had traveled from sun's surface

to heat the earth.

Not a child's geography

of countable circumference, not a map's

correctable surface, but

*a chaos through which its links are for*


the chaining of thoughts to rain, so deeply are they drawn in

through layers of earth.

Put your finger to my lips—
what message
in skin? In asking, the mind, lost to answers, is
*ever and continuously forged.*


The script: *chance summons a chaos*
*through which its links are forever*
*and continuously forged*

UNSCRIPTED / 5

**The given is narrow**

Some days must be stretched thinner than dove-flight, than dollars. Thinned inward toward the interior, not exterior of touch. Thin as sleep, with its purity of witness, an origami crane unfolding its ghosts.

**To ask for generosity**


Despite the tactically derived facsimiles I make of us: parade at the roadside of my eye's narrow perception, an elsewhere banging for entrance, gas stove that clicks warning it's lit, interior air that stings astringent before it thins to punishment, window calk crackling as if the bindings of all things might talk, deep middle of the tongue where everything passes and nothing really touches. Here, right where I've put us: in the space between memory and meaning, between paucity and the pause before plausible. Where any feeling, if felt back, becomes a factory.

**Exposing the seeing: a book of snapshots**


Here is my need to be seen recognizing yours. I am looking out through a window as it loosens its frame and falls toward me like a handkerchief. Here you are, listening to me as if through snow, absorbing only its incorporeal light. Outside, it's rain this morning. Inside, all is isinglass shifting within its stilled surface. Condensation on the image is my witness. No breath finishes where it starts.

**Notes**

All italicized language in this chapbook is quoted from George Bataille's *Eroticism, Death & Sensuality* or *The Tears of Eros*.

*Corporeal Generosity: on Giving with Nietzsche, Merleau-Ponty, and Levinas* by Rosalyn Diprose was an important influence on "Unscripted."

## Acknowledgments

(some poems revised in text and/or title)

The five poems "Assembled from the script," "Sentenced by the script," "Psalm for the script," "Faceless before the script," and "Betoken the script: Bataille" were chosen by John Yau for the Poetry Society of America's 2009 George Bogin Memorial Award. They were subsequently published in *Lana Turner: A Journal of Poetry & Opinion*, No. 2.

*Blue Letter*: "Generosities won't line up to be counted," "Each scene, its own microclimate" and "A distance the given can draw upon"
*Carnet de Route*: "Generosities not easily shared" and "Exposing the seeing: a book of snapshots"
*Colorado Review*: "The given is restive in gesture"
*New American Writing*: "Generosities difficult to discern," "Generosity resists clandestine promises" and "The given confounds"
*Switchback*: "Before generosity is possible, expectation must be abandoned"
*ZYZZYVA*: "To ask for generosity"